WIPE - CLEAN!

ABC

Learn
and write letters
A-Z

**LiTTle
GENIUS
BOOks**

How to use this book

This book will help your child learn the letters of the alphabet in a fun and interactive way.

Sharing activities with your child is a fantastic way to build confidence and have a great time together.

- Find a comfortable place to work.

- Work through the pages in the correct order.

- When tracing the letters, encourage your child to start at the red dot and follow the arrows. If necessary, demonstrate first, then let your child wipe it off and have a go.

- Enjoy the activities together. Point out things around you and talk about the letters they begin with.

- Let your child choose how many pages to complete. If your child gets tired, stop and come back to the same page another time.

- Give lots of encouragement and praise for effort! Remember, mistakes don't matter. Just wipe it off and start again.

- Most important of all, make it fun!

Aa

Apple

Trace the letter.

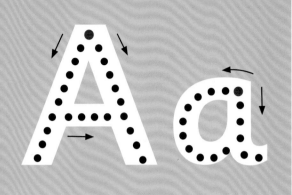

Which one begins with A? Circle it.

Tiger

Penguin

Ant

Now you write it!

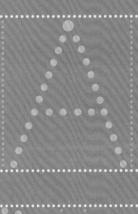

B b

Balloon

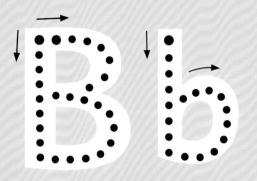

Which one does not begin with B? Circle it.

Bear

Cat

Banana

Now you write it!

B B

b b

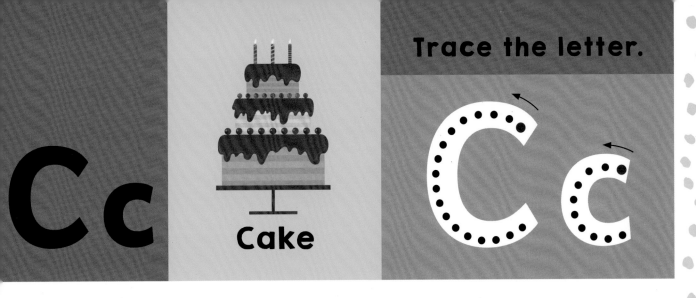

Cc

Cake

Trace the letter.

Which one does not begin with C? Circle it.

Crab　　　　**Car**　　　　**Flamingo**

Now you write it!

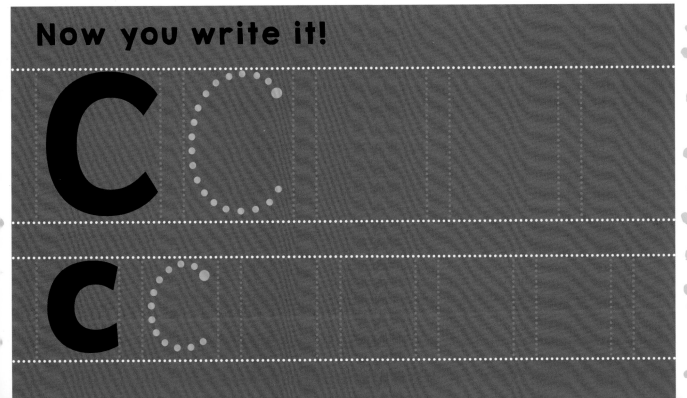

D d

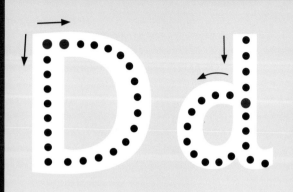

Trace the letter.

Which one begins with D? Circle it.

Donkey

Bell

Camel

Now you write it!

D

d

E e

Elephant

Which one begins with E? Circle it.

Envelope

Dolphin

Snake

Now you write it!

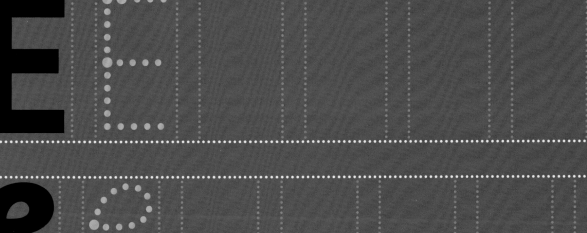

F f

Flower

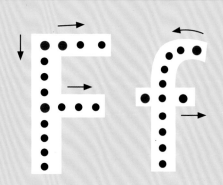

Which one does not begin with F? Circle it.

Frog

Pineapple

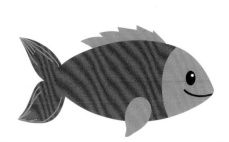

Fish

Now you write it!

G g

Guitar

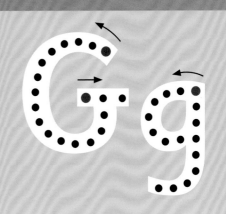

Which one does not begin with G? Circle it.

Goose

Lizard

Grapes

Now you write it!

G

g

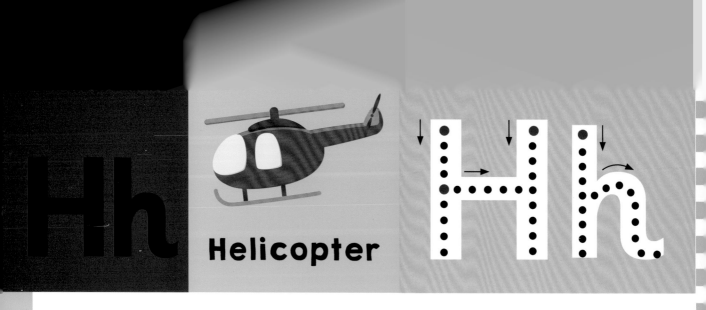

Helicopter

Which one does not begin with H? Circle it.

Hippo   **Hat**   **Raspberry**

Now you write it!

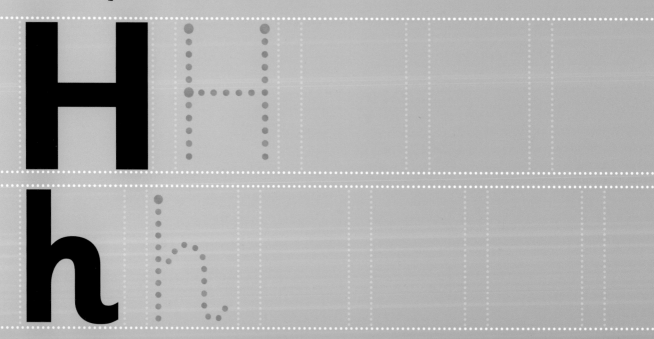

Ii

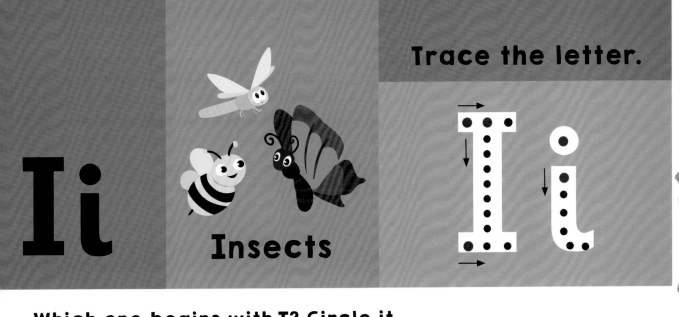

Insects

Trace the letter.

Which one begins with **I**? Circle it.

Iguana   Rhino   Sun

Now you write it!

J j

Jellyfish

Trace the letter.

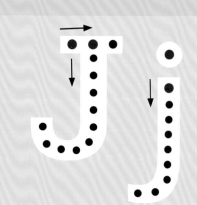

Which one does not begin with J? Circle it.

Jaguar

Juice

Tomato

Now you write it!

J

j

Kk

Kangaroo

Trace the letter.

Kk

Which one begins with K? Circle it.

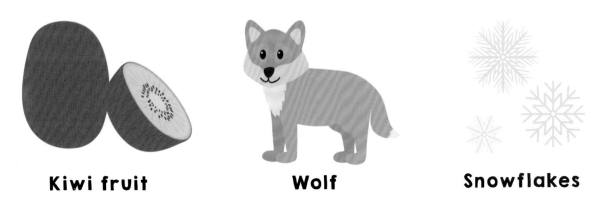

Kiwi fruit   Wolf   Snowflakes

Now you write it!

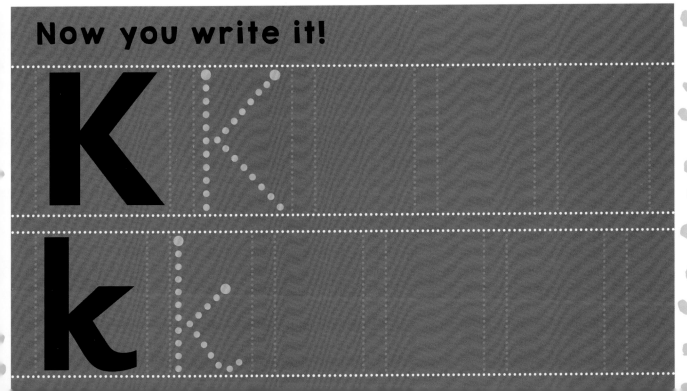

K

k

L l

Lemon

L l

Which one does not begin with L? Circle it.

Lion   Leaf   Racoon

Now you write it!

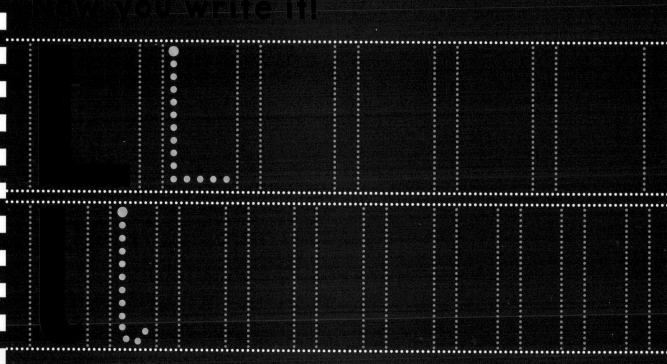

Mm

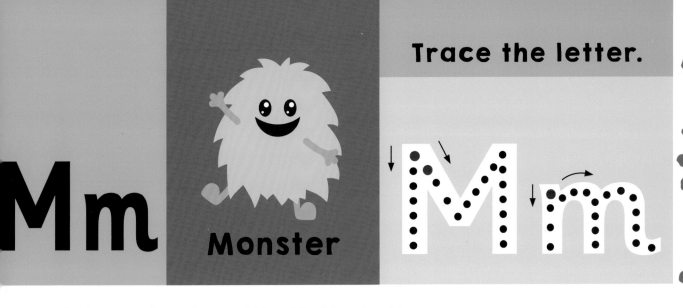

Monster

Trace the letter.

Which one begins with M? Circle it.

Monkey

Yo-yo

Ice cream

Now you write it!

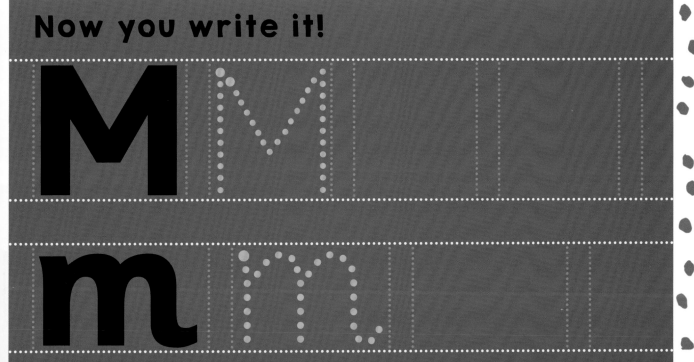

N n

Nut

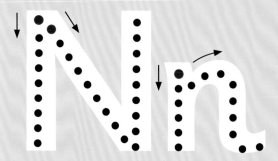

Which one begins with N? Circle it.

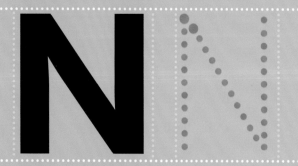

Pig

Nest

Glasses

Now you write it!

Oo

Ostrich

Trace the letter.

Which one does not begin with O? Circle it.

Orange   Octopus   Watermelon

Now you write it!

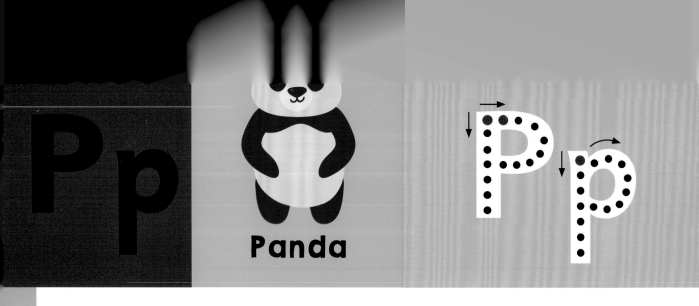

Panda

Which one begins with P? Circle it.

| Pumpkin | Ball | Hummingbird |

Now you write it!

P

p

Qq

Quail

Which one begins with Q? Circle it.

Queen

Dragonfly

Beetle

Now you write it!

Q

q

R r

Rainbow

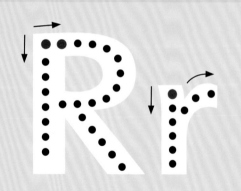

Which one does not begin with R? Circle it.

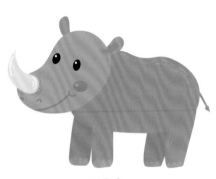

Rocket   Rhino   Snowman

Now you write it!

S s

Strawberry

Which one does not begin with S? Circle it.

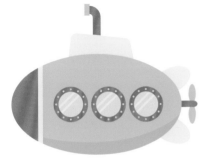

Submarine

Wheel

Skates

Now you write it!

S

S

T t

Train

Trace the letter.

T **t**

Which one begins with T? Circle it.

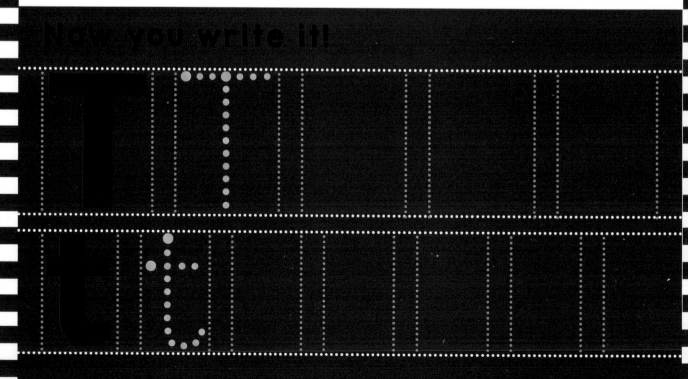

Tiger Worm Horse

Now you write it!

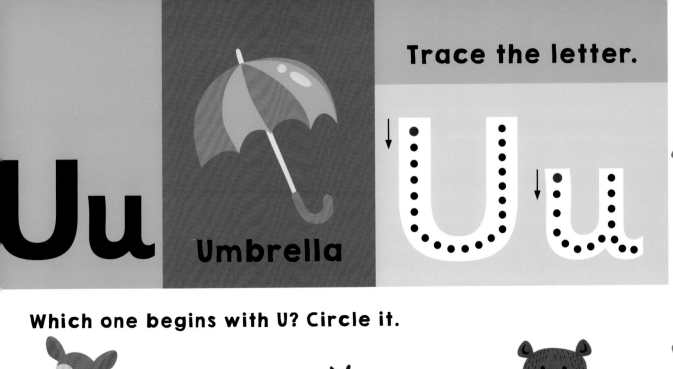

Uu

Umbrella

Trace the letter.

Which one begins with U? Circle it.

Deer

Urchin

Beaver

Now you write it!

V v

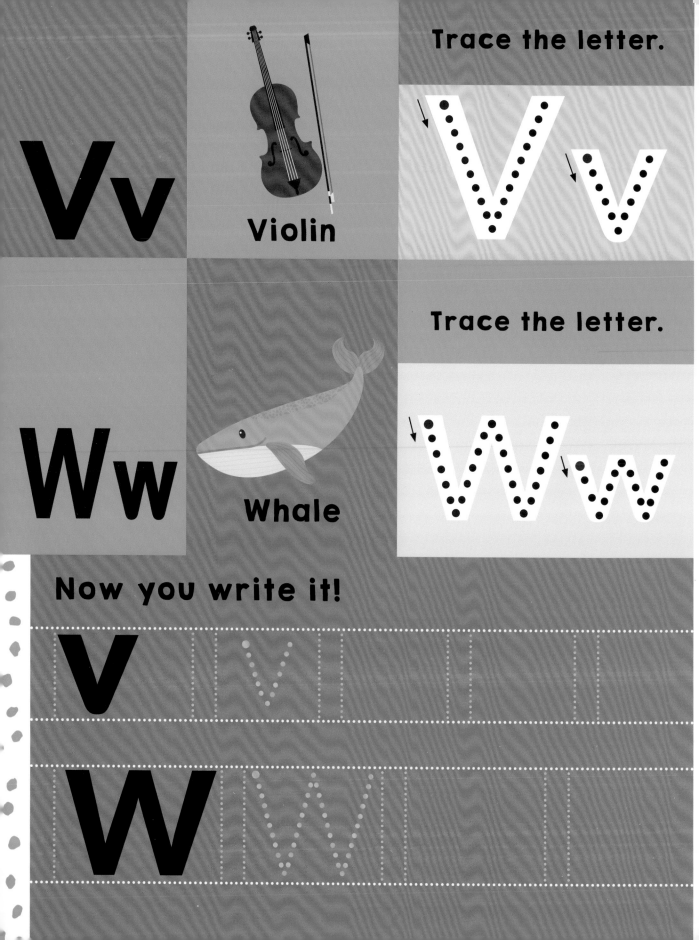

Violin

Trace the letter.

V v

W w

Whale

Trace the letter.

W w

Now you write it!

V

W

X x

X-ray fish

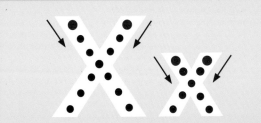

Y y

Yak

Trace the letter.

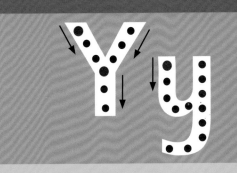

Z z

Zebra

Trace the letter.

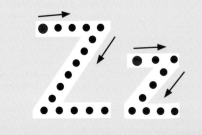

Now you write it!

WRITE IT, WIPE IT!

ABC

Learn and write letters from A to Z.
Each page has dotted guide lines to trace,
plus a fun activity to reinforce letter sounds.

With sturdy pages and a wipe-clean pen, you can have
fun learning again and again!

Little Genius Books
Livingston, NJ 07039, USA
All rights reserved.
© 2021 Curious Universe UK Ltd.
This product conforms to all applicable ASTM and CPSIA standards.
10 9 8 7 6 5 4 3 2 1
Printed in Guangzhou, China, June 2022

$7.99 US / $10.99 CAN
ISBN 9781953344670

www.littlegeniusbooks.com